# Praise for
# Jumpstart Your Job

*Marcia Hall has hit on all the subjects that are essential to your success. If you master all these, you'll be successful in your career.*
Carl Nanney, Former President & CEO, Auto Collision, Inc.

*This is THE handbook everyone wishes they had as they were leaving school. Marcia provides the tips, tricks and success secrets to attaining and keeping the job of your dreams by putting your best foot forward.*
Brenda Bertrand, "The Millennial Coach"

***Jumpstart Your Job** is exactly what I was looking for when I was about to graduate from college. The book is a quick and easy read and told me what employers expect.* Adam Freeze, College of Charleston

*For the past ten years, I have helped managers and employees work more effectively with their bosses, peers, direct reports, and customers. Marcia Hall's book, **Jumpstart Your Job**, contains tips that are invaluable to workers at any level. While the concepts are simple, Marcia presents them in a way that is respectful of the reader and not at all "preachy."*
Wendy Mack, President, T3 Consulting

*The personal attributes Marcia talks about are essential to your ability to succeed. Think of this book as a GPS receiver for navigating you to success in your professional life.*
Pappu Khera, CPA, M.S. Taxation, Khera & Associates, Ltd.

# JUMPSTART
# YOUR JOB

# JUMPSTART YOUR JOB

## 12 Simple Ways to Shift Your Career into High Gear

## Marcia Hall

PARKER
STANTON
PUBLISHING

Severna Park, MD

Published by:
**Parker Stanton Publishing**
PO Box 565
Severna Park, Maryland 21146

Unattributed quotations are by Marcia Hall.

Printed in the United States of America

Library of Congress Control Number: 2007937977

ISBN-13: 978-0-9788066-4-4

Cover design and layout by Steffi Rubin

**Warning-Disclaimer**
The purpose of this book is to educate and entertain. It does not promise or guarantee anyone advancement in one's career by following the suggestions and techniques. This is the right of each employer. The author and Parker Stanton Publishing shall have neither liability nor responsibility to any person or entity with respect to any loss or damage caused, or alleged to have been caused, directly or indirectly, by the information contained in this book.

**Publisher's Note**
Every effort has been made to ensure the accuracy of the information in this book. However, there may be mistakes, both typographical and in content. Furthermore, this book contains information that is current only up to the printing date.

*This book is dedicated to my family and friends,*
*who support and encourage me every day.*

# Contents

Acknowledgments . . . . . . . . . . . . . . . . . . . . . . . . . . . . . . . . . . . . . . . . . . .x

1   The Secret to What Really Counts . . . . . . . . . . . . . . . . . . . . . . . . . . .1

2   What Truly Matters to Employers . . . . . . . . . . . . . . . . . . . . . . . . . .6

3   A Little More about Reputation . . . . . . . . . . . . . . . . . . . . . . . . . . .11

4   Simple Way #1: Very Big Smile . . . . . . . . . . . . . . . . . . . . . . . . . . .16

5   Simple Way #2: "Business Casual"—Decoding the Dress-ups . . . . . .21

6   Simple Way #3: On My Honor . . . . . . . . . . . . . . . . . . . . . . . . . . .26

7   Simple Way #4: Time Travel Still Doesn't Exist . . . . . . . . . . . . . . . .30

8   Simple Way #5: Why "We Try Harder" Is Not Enough . . . . . . . . . . .34

9   Simple Way #6: Can You Hear Me Now? Good . . . . . . . . . . . . . . . .39

10  Simple Way #7: Chew Pride Carefully before Swallowing . . . . . . . .44

11  Simple Way #8: Uh…You're Welcome . . . . . . . . . . . . . . . . . . . . . . .48

12  Simple Way #9: 14AA41 . . . . . . . . . . . . . . . . . . . . . . . . . . . . . . . .51

13  Simple Way #10: What's Your Problem? . . . . . . . . . . . . . . . . . . . . .55

14  Simple Way #11: Staying in Front of the Curve . . . . . . . . . . . . . . . .59

15  Simple Way #12: No, Really—Shut Up! . . . . . . . . . . . . . . . . . . . . .63

16  Let's Meet in Real Life . . . . . . . . . . . . . . . . . . . . . . . . . . . . . . . . .67

17  To Whom It May Concern . . . . . . . . . . . . . . . . . . . . . . . . . . . . . .73

18  Beyond the 12 Simple Ways:
     What Twentysomethings and Employers Said Really Matters . . . . . .79

19  All Done…Bye-bye . . . . . . . . . . . . . . . . . . . . . . . . . . . . . . . . . . . .92

Appendix . . . . . . . . . . . . . . . . . . . . . . . . . . . . . . . . . . . . . . . . . . . . . . . .95

About the Author . . . . . . . . . . . . . . . . . . . . . . . . . . . . . . . . . . . . . . . . .104

# Acknowledgments

While writing this book, I had the great pleasure of talking with wonderful people, including students, new employees, and employers. Their input, stories, and advice helped me tremendously. I want to thank the people who answered my questions and provided suggestions and advice.

Brickman Allen
Yasmin Anderson-Smith
Julie Antinucci
Anne Baber
Rachel Bandarenko
Kara Barnes
Jim Boardman
Kate Boardman
Richard Boardman
Ryan Bricklemeyer
Sharon Cager
Matthew Clarke
Kyle Clelan
Patina Copeland
Teresa Divers
Shelly DonBullian
Nancy Dowen
Jessie Dulaney
Bailey Dunn
Ronald Edmund
Ryan Elkins
Nancy Fink
William Franz
Adam Freeze
James Fulks

Julia Galeazzi
Josh Garvey
Gary Geisel
Ross Geisel
Savanna Grotz
Benjamin Hall
Christopher Hall
Geoffrey Hall
Jennifer Hall
Dane Hanson
Tiffany Harris
Sallie Hays
Geoffrey Johnson
Jennifer Keiser
Stacey Koons
Meghan Kwasniak
Scott Laughlin
Cait Lecksell
Victoria Lee
Kim Leisey, PhD
Katrina Leitkowski
Anne Logie
Cheryl Lucas
Kelli McDonough
Kristi McDurmon

Mary McMurtry
Jaime Mendez
Laura Mistretta
Amy Moreland
Carl Nanney
Lavenia Nesmith
Gary Palmieri
Lydia Potter
Christine Renner
Kaely Roe
Lucas Roe
Pullak Rozario
Elan Schnitzer
Anne Scholl-Fiedler
Jena Siegel
Christen Skiff
Martha Smith, PhD
Lynne Stanton
Jmahl Stewart
Jennifer Stillings
James Valentine
Scott Wallace
Lynne Waymon

Special thanks goes to the people who helped me with the editing process.

# 1

# The Secret to What Really Counts

**Did you know that 80% of employees who lose their jobs do so because of poor work ethics?**

According to the U.S. Department of Labor, the lack of occupational skills was not the reason these workers were fired. Instead, they did not have the *interpersonal skills* that employers expect.

Another startling statistic is that 46% of newly-hired employees will fail within 18 months, according to a study by Leadership IQ. Employers will tell you it is because these new hires aren't motivated, have a poor attitude, or can't accept feedback.

These workers do not know the secret to what really counts. Do you?

## The Secret to What Really Counts

It is your *everyday behavior.*

If you demonstrate the personal attributes that employers want, they will learn they can count on you.

In reality, your everyday behavior, which is something you choose to do and is therefore in your control, creates a perception in people's minds about who you are. This perception becomes your reputation.

If it is good, employers think of you when opportunities arise or it's time to promote someone. If it is bad, you probably won't get challenging projects. You may even be shown the door.

Whether you are a new employee or have been on the job for some time, how you act in the workplace will help or hinder your career.

## How Can You Learn the Skills Employers Value?

Employers always want their workers to demonstrate certain behaviors, sometimes called "soft skills." Many employees do not understand that their success depends on consistently demonstrating these behaviors.

> It simply does not matter what job or career you have chosen. It has nothing to do with how old you are. You can do certain things to make you stand apart. If you do them and someone older does not, you get the edge.

*Jumpstart Your Job* tells you how to develop universal behaviors most all employers value. Twelve of the most important are covered in this book.

What are they? Here is a preview of the **12 Simple Ways:**

#1: Very Big Smile
#2: "Business Casual"—Decoding the Dress-ups
#3: On My Honor
#4: Time Travel Still Doesn't Exist
#5: Why "We Try Harder" Is Not Enough
#6: Can You Hear Me Now? Good
#7: Chew Pride Carefully Before Swallowing

#8:    Uh… You're Welcome
#9:    14AA41
#10:   What's Your Problem?
#11:   Staying in Front of the Curve
#12:   No, Really—Shut Up!

Once you read about these simple ways, you may think each one is a no-brainer. You might think they are too obvious. You might say, "Of course, I do them." In reality, most people practice only a few or do not do them consistently.

The new employees I interviewed told me they wish they had been aware of how important these behaviors were *before* starting their first jobs. In an Introduction to Management course at UMBC, I talked to college students about reputation building and the simple ways. One senior expressed the consensus of the class. She said, "Developing and demonstrating these skills is everything. They will make or break your career."

*Jumpstart Your Job* tells you what you need to do to succeed, wherever you are in your career. You can be one who knows the "secret that really counts."

## How This Book Helps You

Employers and employees will be quoted from various industries—large and small—to tell you what you can do to build a reputation to help you move your career forward. While there are no guarantees, your odds greatly improve when you establish a stellar reputation.

The point of this book is to be short, practical, and not overwhelming so you will read and practice the behaviors on the job.

It tells you in plain English what traits matter most in the workplace. The best part is that developing these attributes does not cost anything.

*I think that someone who shows up every day, works hard, gives their best, and never says no is better than 75 percent of the working public. Very few people, especially my generation, do not use all of their sick days, find ample opportunities to surf the Internet, take longer lunches, leave at 4:59, and generally try to do enough work just to get by. By this theory, anything above that really puts you into a group of elite employees.*

—National Nonprofit Analyst

## My Qualifications to Write about Personal Reputation

*If you could describe the work ethics and credibility of anyone as superior, it would be Marcia.* Geoffrey Johnson, Nationwide Insurance, President of the West Anne Arundel County Chamber of Commerce, quoted in an article in the *Maryland Gazette*, November 1995

*Perhaps her greatest legacy is how she was able to bring area businesses and schools together as a team to improve the quality of life in our community.* Our Say: Editor's Notebook, *West County News*, and *The Capital*, April 5, 2001, upon Marcia Hall's retirement from the West Anne Arundel County Chamber of Commerce

*Marcia Hall is a gifted professional and a wonderful advocate for educational and professional development opportunities.* Martha A. Smith, PhD, President, Anne Arundel Community College

I credit the **12 Simple Ways** in this book for my success. When you demonstrate personal attributes that employers want, you build the type of reputation that moves your career forward.

Certainly, there are more than 12, but the ones I have selected will serve you well if you practice them consistently. The type of job you have now and in the future will not matter because employers in all industries desire these behaviors.

Simply put, reputation counts.

# 2

# What Truly Matters to Employers

*You hire attitude; everything else can be trained.*
Herb Kelleher, Cofounder, Chairman and Former CEO,
Southwest Airlines

## Down in the Trenches

What are the desired behaviors that employers want to see in their employees? Who better to ask than supervisors who interact with workers every day.

It was noteworthy that I heard the same responses—whether it was a large corporation or small business. This is exactly what I was looking for. What traits are desired universally—without regard to a person's age, gender, experience, or type of business?

Each company or organization has its own expectations, which cannot possibly be covered here. Instead, this book talks about the universal attributes that employers care about most.

## Do You Have What It Takes?

Of course, employers want to know that you have occupational and technical skills, particularly computer competence. If you are a new graduate, they will look at your academic records and work experience.

Activities outside of school are also important, particularly if you have been in leadership roles.

Employers want people who can get along. They need to know you will fit in with other employees and be a team player.

Very importantly, employers want to know that what you do contributes to the bottom line.

In focus groups, students were asked what they thought employers cared about the most. They said:

- Productivity
- Ability to work a full workday
- Dependability
- Ability to adapt and adjust to the work environment
- Choice of attire
- Past work experience
- Customer service skills
- Honesty
- Communication skills
- Ability to work well with coworkers
- Ability to stay with a job for the long term

Multiple studies show that employers do indeed care about the attributes listed by the students.

Ranked first in many surveys is the ability to communicate effectively, including speaking, writing, and listening. Because there are many excellent books about communication skills with several listed in the Appendix, they will not be covered in depth. Instead, we will focus on the less tangible attributes, which are highly desired as well. Among those cited most often are:

## Positive Attitude
- Positive attitude and enthusiasm for work
- Friendly
- Sense of humor
- Self-confidence

## Professionalism
- Acts and looks professional
- Knows how to respond (Demonstrates maturity)
- Controls emotions

## Responsibility
- Dependable and reliable (Can the employer count on you?)
- Does job well, regardless of what it is
- Takes responsibility for actions
- Solves problems
- Proactive
- Self-starter
- Inspires trust

## Work Ethic
- Delivers work on time
- Does what it takes to get the job done
- Planning and time management skills
- Ability to work independently

## Integrity/Honesty
- Does the right thing
- Ability to admit mistakes and seek solutions
- Does not blame others
- Is truthful

## Respect
- Respectful of others (Treats people well)
- Sensitive to cultural diversity
- Demonstrates loyalty to company

## Leadership
- Team player
- Motivates and helps others
- Takes risks and shows initiative
- Self-starter

## Adaptability
- Being flexible (Accepts and adapts to change)
- Interest in learning new information and skills
- Knows how to follow
- Takes directions well

With such a long list of desired attributes, I talked to the following workforce development representatives. They have years of experience in understanding what employers value. I wanted to see if they could identify some priorities:

Sharon Cager and William Franz
Business Resource Representatives
One-Stop Career Center
Maryland Workforce Exchange

Sallie Hays
Industry Initiative Coordinator
Governor's Workforce Investment Board
Maryland Department of Labor, Licensing and Regulation

Scott Wallace
Special Projects Manager
Anne Arundel Workforce Development Corporation

They narrowed the list of desired qualities to those they thought people should develop. These include:

- Being enthusiastic and having a positive attitude
- Being responsible, being on time, and working hard
- Having decent communication skills
- Being honest
- Being willing to learn and ask questions

In the following chapters, you will learn why these attributes are so important to your success.

# 3

# A Little More About Reputation

*When you're 20, you don't think that your*
*behavior will matter later. It 100 percent matters.*
*At some point, it's going to bite you.*
Shelly DonBullian
Owner, Curves of Dunkirk

## What Is Reputation?

If you look up the definition of reputation, one of the meanings is simply "a good name." If you look up "reputation" in the thesaurus, you'll find wonderful words, including:

- Trustworthy
- Upright
- Reliable
- Principled
- Creditable
- Estimable
- Unimpeachable
- Honorable
- Respectable
- Dependable
- Good
- Worthy
- Irreproachable
- Excellent

Who wouldn't want those words used to describe himself or herself? Who wouldn't want to be known as honorable, trustworthy, or principled?

## The Other Side

But there is another side to reputation. What if you are known for being unreliable or dishonest? What kinds of feelings do those words generate? It takes many years to build an exemplary reputation, but just one act can destroy—or at least negatively impact—that reputation.

Think of an athlete who has tested positive for steroid use. He denies it, but you might now wonder about his previous accomplishments. What will be the first thing you think about when hearing that athlete's name again? Whether or not that athlete ever regains his good reputation is in doubt. It could take years, if it happens at all.

## Business and Reputation

Businesses understand the importance of reputation. Many hire reputation management firms as part of their public relations strategy. These companies want to be known for consistency, value, and being trustworthy.

Think of Microsoft, Starbucks, or Johnson & Johnson. We know we can rely on the company's name to consistently produce a product of value.

## Personal Reputation

The same is true for people. Employers who are in a position to send opportunities your way will notice that you are trustworthy and consistently doing a good job.

If you are already in the workplace, it is important to know what people think of you and where you need to improve. For example, if you make a mistake, what is the reaction from your boss and/or coworker? Do they cut you some slack? Or, are they secretly pleased? A lot depends on the reputation you have established. If it is good, you may hear supportive comments. If it is bad, they may abandon you.

In his book, *The World is Flat,* Thomas Friedman talks about how the Internet has opened access to information worldwide. You can Google everything. That means you can never escape your reputation. Mr. Friedman, a Pulitzer Prize winner and columnist for *The New York Times,* spoke with Dov Seidman, founder and CEO of LRN, a firm that provides business ethics and legal compliance solutions. Mr. Seidman was quoted as saying that students "don't get to spend four years getting drunk." Potential employers now have a way to find out about that type of reputation.

Employers want to know as much as they can before they hire you. Anything online, particularly "digital dirt," will probably come to their attention. It could hurt your chances of getting the job you want. Even before you have interviewed for the job, you already have a reputation in their eyes.

## Self-Assessment

Before reading about the **12 Simple Ways,** it is good to see where you are right now.

**On a scale of 0 to 5, with 5 being something you do all the time, rate yourself on the following actions:**

| | |
|---|---|
| Do you smile when you greet people? | 0 1 2 3 4 5 |
| Do you look people in the eye when speaking to them? | 0 1 2 3 4 5 |
| Do you consider what might be appropriate dress before you go out? | 0 1 2 3 4 5 |
| Do you get work or school assignments done on time? | 0 1 2 3 4 5 |
| Are you on time to your job, class, a study group, or club meeting? | 0 1 2 3 4 5 |

| | |
|---|---|
| Do you return non-sales phone calls and e-mails no more than 12 to 24 hours later? | 0 1 2 3 4 5 |
| Do you admit your mistakes? | 0 1 2 3 4 5 |
| Do you use proper grammar and avoid slang in a work or school setting? | 0 1 2 3 4 5 |
| Do you write thank-you notes? | 0 1 2 3 4 5 |
| Do you say thank you when someone does something for you? | 0 1 2 3 4 5 |
| Are you asked for your opinion? | 0 1 2 3 4 5 |
| Do you avoid complaining? | 0 1 2 3 4 5 |
| Do you avoid gossiping? | 0 1 2 3 4 5 |
| Do you help others, even when you would rather do something else? | 0 1 2 3 4 5 |
| Do your friends or coworkers ask you for help? | 0 1 2 3 4 5 |
| Do you stop yourself from interrupting other people while they are speaking? | 0 1 2 3 4 5 |
| Do you actually hear what other people say before you respond? | 0 1 2 3 4 5 |
| Do other people ask you to be their mentor? | 0 1 2 3 4 5 |
| If you do not know how to do something that would make life easier for you, do you make it a priority to learn the skill you need? | 0 1 2 3 4 5 |
| Do you keep your word when you make a promise to do something? | 0 1 2 3 4 5 |
| **TOTAL** | |

## Scoring Your Assessment

| | |
|---|---|
| 80–100 | Fabulous! Read this book. Then pass it along to friends, or reread when you need a boost. |
| 60–79 | You are already headed in the right direction. Practice the **12 Simple Ways** for even more success. |
| 40–59 | You are in the middle of the pack, and there are lots of ways to move up. Read on. |
| 20–39 | Some red flags are being raised. Fortunately, by reading this book, you are catching them now. |
| 0–19 | Help is on the way! Carefully read and practice the **12 Simple Ways.** |

You will have the opportunity to take this assessment again once you go through the **12 Simple Ways.**

> *I was not the best employee then. Now I understand the mistakes, and they can really stick with you. I was lucky to start being involved in the community as an adult, so I didn't have a past reputation to haunt me. I see people still struggling to live down, trying to mend something they did earlier.*
>
> Shelly DonBullian, owner of a Curves franchise
> reflecting on her years in college

Right now, ask yourself, "What do people think about me first when they hear my name? Can they count on me, or not?"

In the following chapters, you will learn how to build your reputation. Each simple way will be explained, and you will hear why employers care about them. That will be followed by simple action steps with a start date.

I suggest you work on one simple way at a time until you can do it without thinking about it. It may take one week or one month. Master each one before moving on.

There is an area for notes in each chapter, too. Write down your progress so you can track your success.

# 4

# Simple Way #1
# Very Big Smile

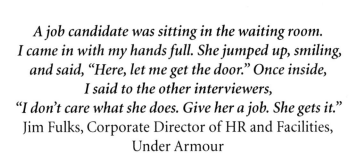

*A job candidate was sitting in the waiting room.*
*I came in with my hands full. She jumped up, smiling,*
*and said, "Here, let me get the door." Once inside,*
*I said to the other interviewers,*
*"I don't care what she does. Give her a job. She gets it."*
Jim Fulks, Corporate Director of HR and Facilities,
Under Armour

Last year, I wrote a story for a local newspaper about what attributes employers wanted in their workers.

Every time I survey employers, the results are the same. There is one trait that is mentioned most often; employers want their workers to have a positive attitude.

According to the businesspeople I interviewed, technical skills are not nearly as important as attitude and desire. Carl Nanney, former president and CEO of Auto Collision, Inc., said, "I can't teach you how to be a nice guy or have the desire to do the work."

Another employer was blunt in her comments about some of her new employees. "As a rule, I don't get the impression that they care," she said. "It's their body language, the comments they make, or their lack of enthusiasm."

## Likeability

Being likeable is clearly an essential component of your ability to get and keep the job. Tim Sanders wrote an entire book on this subject in *The Likeability Factor: How to Boost Your L-Factor and Achieve Your Life's Dreams*. Your attitude, enthusiasm, and sincerity cause an employer to think, "I like him or her."

How do you know this about a person? One big way is to physically display these attributes. A simple way is to smile. Don't use a fake, fawning expression. Give a genuine smile.

Kaely Roe is a 20-year-old college student and the owner of Severna Perk Coffeehouse in Severna Park, Maryland. Kaely knows many of her customers by name. Friendly smiles on faces of all the staff is the norm at the coffeehouse.

Kaely told me about a situation that could have potentially lost her many customers if it wasn't for the positive approach she used. "I was by myself. The store was filled with people, with the line stretching all the way to the door. I remembered a trick I learned about talking to the whole group at once. I told them to grab a newspaper or talk to their neighbor, just like they learned in kindergarten. Everyone laughed, and the whole feeling in the room changed. I didn't lose one customer."

## What Happens When You Aren't Likeable

We have all seen people who consistently frown. Do you have any desire to be around such a person? People who appear to be gloomy get a reputation for that negativity.

One employer told me about a worker who was highly skilled and productive, but he could not stand being around other people. He rarely smiled and seldom interacted with coworkers. The tension his behavior produced finally convinced the employer to let the worker go.

"I should have dealt with this much earlier," the employer said. "It finally came down to his unfriendly attitude being more important than his productivity."

There is no room for a "bad day" attitude at work. Employers, while they may be sympathetic, do not have any tolerance for people who bring moodiness to the workplace. You have to check that at the door. You can never bring it to work and expect that your reputation will not suffer, particularly if this is a regular habit for you.

> *Work is work. Home is home.*
> William Franz

Knowing how to shake hands is also essential. You don't want to use a wimpy or fishlike grip or shake hands too forcefully. Use a firm handshake instead. Look people in the eyes when you shake hands and/or talk to them. While these acts are very basic in nature, they are critically important and too often forgotten.

The following are some tips for handshakes and eye contact:

## Handshakes
a.   Avoid a wimpy or too forceful handshake.
b.   Use a confident, friendly handshake. Look the person in the eye. Grasp firmly. Pump up and down a couple of times.

c. Always extend your hand when greeting another person. There are no rules about who does it first. When introductions are made, stand up, unless you are in an environment where it is difficult to do so.

### Eye Contact

a. Avoid looking away often, especially as new people enter the room. Do not look over the shoulder of the person to whom you are talking.
b. Look directly at the person for seven to eight seconds before looking away. Then glance to the side, not over his or her shoulder. If it is difficult for you, you do not have to always look people directly in the eye. Look at an eyebrow or the nose.

These guidelines are used in the United States. If you work in another country, you'll want to be aware of local customs.

Employees who understand the power of a positive attitude most definitely have an edge. They understand that people want to work and do business with other people they like.

"Attitude is simply a big one," Carl Nanney said. "It's way up there on the list."

## SUMMARY

- A positive attitude can be demonstrated through smiling, extending your hand, and making eye contact.
- Employers want to hire and work with people they like.
- Leave personal problems at home.

## What Attribute This Simple Way Demonstrates
* Positive Attitude

## Why Employers Want This
* It demonstrates you can get along with others.
* They can trust you to represent the company well.

# SIMPLE ACTION STEPS

**Start Date:**_____

1. On the job, practice smiling at all clients, customers, bosses, and coworkers on a daily basis.
2. If you are in school, smile at professors, students, and other people on campus on a daily basis.
3. As you meet new people socially, take the opportunity to practice smiling. Extend your hand, and maintain eye contact. You never know if this person might be a potential resource down the line.
4. Read *The Likeability Factor: How to Boost Your L-Factor and Achieve Your Life's Dreams* by Tim Sanders. It shows you how to develop the art of being friendly.

Notes _____

_____

_____

_____

_____

_____

_____

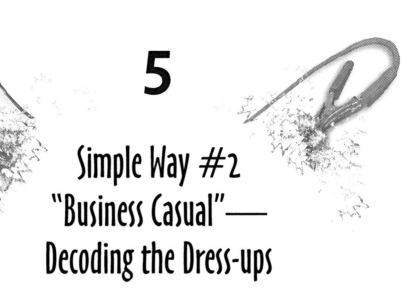

# 5

# Simple Way #2 "Business Casual"— Decoding the Dress-ups

*Wearing clothes that are too trendy may send the*
*wrong message or cost you your job.*
Yasmin Anderson-Smith,
Image and Brand Management
Consultant, KYMS Image International LLC

Employees often have questions about what is acceptable to wear to work.

"Younger workers think they are dressing up when they wear trendy clothes," Meghan Kwasniak, a manager with Laureate Education Inc., said. "They believe it's okay as long as it's not excluded in the dress code."

According to Jim Fulks, corporate director of HR and Facilities with Under Armour, employees need to understand unwritten rules regarding appropriate dress.

"You dress up to start with, look around and see what others are wearing, and conform if you are dressing differently," Jim said. "It's not written down. You just get it. Your reputation is at stake."

Jim talked about an employee at a hotel where he previously worked. She appeared to be very skilled in the interview and wore appropriate business attire. But she wore miniskirts on the job. There was a lot of gossiping, and nobody spoke to her about it.

She soon was not getting enough challenging work or responsibilities because her appearance was influencing how people felt about her. They stopped trusting her, and this situation disrupted the workplace. After 90 days, she was let go.

In school, dressing up may mean putting on your trendy clothes. But appropriate dress in the workplace is often very different. Your clothes determine how professional you appear. According to all employers I surveyed, professionalism is highly desired in their employees.

People form an impression about you when they observe your dress. The good news is that you have control over this by observing others and carefully deciding what you will wear.

"I think one of the biggest problems is that people coming out of school don't know how to dress in business situations," said Kaely Roe. "Girls wear very inappropriate stuff. Dressed up for work is not the same thing as dressed up when you go to a club," she said.

Kaely advised to not "break the bank" when you shop for clothes for work. Instead, make sure you buy quality clothing.

"Don't forget to shower and use deodorant. If you wear perfume or cologne, use just a little," she cautioned, even though those might be obvious points. "If you don't, it turns anybody off."

An important part of your appearance is your hairstyle. Lavenia Nesmith, vocational rehabilitation supervisor with the Maryland State Department of Education, recalled an experience that changed her beliefs about the impact a hairstyle can have.

"Several years ago I interviewed for a position with a major corporation," Lavenia said. "A friend of mine who worked there told me about the opening, but expressed the opinion that I probably wouldn't get the job because of my haircut. I had decided to cut my hair very short because I was exercising a lot, even running marathons, and I didn't want to be bothered by it.

"My friend suggested that I wear a wig. I told him no because it wasn't who I was. It would have been deceiving, and anyway, I was qualified and always dressed in a professional manner. I thought I was sharp looking and chic.

"The day of the interview I felt prepared and confident. However, as soon as I walked in the door, there was no mistaking their surprise. Their eyes went to my hair. I thought to myself, 'Oh, crap. My friend is right.' The interview went well, however, and they spent a lot of time with me so I thought my haircut didn't affect them after all.

"The next day my friend called. He told me they were very impressed with me in the interview, but I wouldn't get the job.

"'Your image didn't fit the culture,' my friend explained. 'They felt threatened by it and perceived you as radical and militant.' In a few days, I received a call from the company representative who told me they had found someone more 'suitable.'

"I later came to realize that my haircut was extreme and that I had the responsibility to present an image the company needed. It was my hair that did me in. And yet this experience was not enough to totally convince me. Within a year, it happened again. I was sitting in the airport and the man next to me said, 'I bet men have a problem with you.'

"I said, 'Excuse me? Why did you say that? You don't know me.'

"'It's your hair,' he replied. 'It conveys a message.'

"'What's the message?' I asked.

"'That you don't give a damn,' he said.

"Through these two experiences I realized that not only is attire important, but so is the hairstyle. I was made to pay attention to the reality that your appearance must be compatible with the company culture. There is no escaping the fact that to be perceived seriously, you must conform to the expectations in each workplace environment."

It's not only your hair that matters. For example, wearing a nose stud or displaying a tattoo may not fit the company culture. Fortunately, those types of accessories are totally in your control.

## SUMMARY

- Trendy clothes may not be appropriate in your workplace.
- Conform to what is being worn by coworkers.
- Understand what is acceptable in your company.
- People will judge you by your appearance.

### What Attribute This Simple Way Demonstrates
- Professionalism

### Why Employers Want This
- Professional appearance is important to demonstrate to clients and customers.
- You are a representative of the company.
- Employees seem more committed.

# SIMPLE ACTION STEPS

Start Date:_____

1. Start observing how people dress in offices and other professional settings, for example, banks, insurance agencies, and accounting or law firms.
2. Attend a "Dress for Success" workshop.
3. Talk with people in your field about appropriate dress.
4. Read *Casual Power: How to Power Up Your Nonverbal Communication and Dress Down for Success* by Sherry Maysonave. The book has pictures of what business casual means for both men and women.
5. Assess your wardrobe to determine what clothing you need to acquire. If finances are an issue, take advantage of sales and outlets.

Notes _____

_____

_____

_____

_____

_____

_____

_____

_____

_____

_____

_____

_____

_____

# 6

# Simple Way #3
# On My Honor

*"Do what you say you will do" is the ultimate
obligation. Your word is number one.*
Carl Nanney, Former President & CEO,
Auto Collision, Inc.

During my years at the chamber of commerce, I worked with hundreds of businesspeople. Carl Nanney was one of the first people I met. He ran a very successful auto repair facility in Maryland. Over the years, I have come to greatly respect him as the owner of a top-notch business and for his integrity.

Carl served on many chamber committees, and his word was gold. He would never commit to more than he could do. That was not always the case with other members.

"I'll make sure the report gets to everyone before the next meeting," a member would say.

At the next meeting, we'd hear, "I was very busy this past month, and I didn't have a chance to write the report."

How often have you heard that yourself? How many times has a coworker or student on your team project let you down?

> *At my internship last summer, I was involved in a group competition among all the interns. When I found out the members of my group, I was really disappointed because I had not seen any of them produce good work.*
>
> 24-year-old graduate student

People often commit to things they later realize they cannot do. They believe other people are grateful for them taking on so much and will understand if they cannot do it all. They do not grasp that people form a negative impression of them instead. They are tagged as unreliable, and that impression will probably stick. Nothing that person does will easily erase the over-promising that he/she did.

If you miss a deadline, employers don't care what excuse you use. They simply want the work to get done. A true emergency might be the exception, but not necessarily, particularly if you are in the habit of using excuses frequently.

Excuses are often used when people don't want to do something or haven't allowed enough time to accomplish the task. Matthew Clarke, a manager with New York Life Insurance Company, said that as a child he learned it was, "more work to get out of work than to just do it."

"When I was a kid, my dad asked me to sweep the cellar," Matthew said. "It would have taken me 10 minutes to do it, but I goofed off for four hours instead. Later, my dad pointed out that I used a lot of energy to waste four hours. If I had swept the cellar right away, I would have had the rest of that time to do what I really wanted.

"Even today I fall into that trap. While I have a 'To Do' list every day, I sometimes pick out the easy things to do and goof off mentally with some of the others. That wasted time cuts into my open time for me and my family. To help me get back on track, I'm a big planner. I write down what I need to do and when I'll do it."

> **The key is to promise a little and then deliver a lot.**

As mentioned earlier, Shelly DonBullian is the owner of a Curves franchise in Dunkirk, Maryland. With some 9,000 locations, Curves is the world's largest fitness franchise. Shelly does not make promises she cannot keep, and her employees practice this as well.

"I have a manager who sometimes renders me speechless," Shelly said. "If she promises a member something, she follows through immediately. If I ask her to take care of paperwork or contact someone, she does it, and I only have to ask once."

One of the manager's responsibilities is to ensure the facility is open at 7:00 am. "She makes sure that is done—even when she is sick," Shelly said.

This manager is following the belief that you must be responsible for your obligations. In turn, Shelly, her boss, acknowledges her behavior. In fact, Shelly noticed it so much that this manager came to mind first when we talked about responsibility.

## SUMMARY

- Keep your word.
- Do whatever you say you will do by the agreed-upon deadline.
- Underpromise and overdeliver.

### What Attributes This Simple Way Demonstrates
- Responsibility
- Work Ethic
- Integrity

## Why Employers Want This

- It demonstrates you are dependable.
- They do not have to stand over your shoulder.
- They can count on you when things get hectic, and their stress levels will not increase by wondering if you will come through.

# SIMPLE ACTION STEPS

Start Date:_____

1. On the job, get work done on time—without excuses. While you're at it, add a smile.
2. If you are in school and working on a class project with other students, clearly state what you will do, and deliver it by the deadline—without excuses.
3. For a social occasion, if you agree to invite friends by a certain date or get food, make sure you do it. Take on only as much as you are certain you will do.

Notes_____

_____

_____

_____

_____

_____

_____

_____

_____

_____

_____

# 7

## Simple Way #4
## Time Travel Still Doesn't Exist

*Being on time is late. You have to be early. If you show up*
*three minutes late, we needed you three minutes ago.*
Mary McMurtry, Former Regional Manager Field
Employment, Southwest Airlines

Perhaps one of the deadliest mistakes you can make (and most costly to your reputation) is being late. Even once can cause people to wonder about you.

When I talked with employers, they were dismayed that so many job seekers were late for interviews. On the job, it is one behavior for which they have little tolerance.

Nancy Dowen is a college student and a Starbucks lead, that is, manager. She has been on the job for five years and a manager for the last two. When asked what she looked for in her employees, Nancy identified important characteristics as being enthusiastic, having good rapport with customers, and being mature. But one behavior was essential.

"Be on time," she stated. "That's the biggest thing."

You probably know people who are always late. Have you experienced any of these?

- Your friend comes 30 minutes late every time you make plans.
- You are part of a team that meets weekly and one of the members arrives one hour late each week.
- Club meetings consistently start late because the president is never on time.

Do you have a favorable impression of these people? It is more likely that their actions annoy you. If you are the person who is always late, you become known as unreliable. Once you have such a reputation, it is extremely difficult to change that perception.

Through their research, business networking experts Anne Baber and Lynne Waymon, authors of *Make Your Contacts Count*, talk about the "All or Nothing Rule."

## All or Nothing Rule

*If you do something well, people assume you do everything well.*
*If you do something wrong, people assume you do nothing well.*

By always being late, you demonstrate something wrong. Your boss may leap to the conclusion that you are also a slacker and incompetent.

Recently, CareerBuilder.com surveyed employers to find out what they thought about workers being late. One of the statistics really caught my attention:

**"One-in-five managers say they might fire an employee who is late three times *in a year*."**

You may find this hard to believe, particularly if an employee is getting his work done. However, the boss starts to wonder, "Can I depend on this employee to be there when I need him?" It becomes an issue of trust.

Being late shows a lack of respect and implies that you value your time more than the other person's. If you are frequently late, your credibility and reputation will suffer.

But if you consistently come early or arrive on time, people learn that they can count on you. This is expected in the workplace, but not everyone understands its importance. It is a very easy way to shine on the job every day.

> *No show, no call—you resign.*
> One company's policy

## SUMMARY

- Be on time or early for everything.
- Excuses will not be tolerated.

### What Attributes This Simple Way Demonstrates
- Responsibility
- Respect

### Why Employers Want This
- It demonstrates you are reliable.
- It shows you take your job seriously.
- It indicates you have a responsible attitude.

# SIMPLE ACTION STEPS

**Start Date:**_____

1. On the job, start arriving early. Set your alarm to give yourself the time.
2. If you are in school, start arriving to class early. Let your professors see you.
3. If you are in college, no later than your senior year, schedule at least one early morning class. Consistently show up. Even though one of the pleasures of college is the ability to select classes when you want to take them, if you do not get in the habit of getting up early and ready to work, it can be quite a hurdle to overcome once you get a job.
4. Make a point of attending a club or team project meeting and dates with friends when you say you will be there. Be consistent.

Notes_____

_____

_____

_____

_____

_____

_____

_____

_____

_____

_____

_____

_____

# 8

## Simple Way #5
## Why "We Try Harder"
## is Not Enough

*I know the people I can count on.*
*If I go out of town for a week, I know the place will be okay.*
*Those people will go beyond their normal tasks.*
Kaely Roe, Owner, Severna Perk

One afternoon, Kaely and I talked about employees who demonstrate something beyond their job description.

"Everyone is given responsibilities," she said. "If you go beyond that, you are paid more, and you stay longer. You are happier, and you enjoy working here. Employees who just stick to the responsibilities usually fade and leave.

"Most of my employees don't see it as just a job," she continued. "Rather, it is an entity that is being pushed forward. We want to see it succeed."

William Franz, business resource representative with the One-Stop Career Center in Maryland, agreed that employees who think about the company first really do have an edge.

"What gets you that promotion?" he asked. "It's being flexible, willing to go the extra mile, staying late when needed, and going beyond the job description."

At first glance, it may seem that this simple way is the same as #3 (On My Honor). But the simple way in this chapter takes it one step further.

Not only do you need to get the tasks done, you must consistently do your best work and even exceed expectations. In fact, "I'll try my best" just does not cut it.

> *My first job was with ABC News. In the news industry, the office doesn't close! I made it known that I was willing to work overtime and take on additional projects. Weekends, early mornings, late nights. I would do it, and it was worth it!*
>
> Meghan Kwasniak

To move ahead, you must:
- Do what it takes as well as the time you need to get the job done.
- Get it done well.
- Anticipate what might be needed next, or determine how to solve problems before they occur.

### Effort is not the same as excellence and execution.

People who excel and execute are tagged for promotion. They consistently do what it takes. In other words, they may have to stay late at work or come in on a weekend. Their priority is getting the job done—without complaint.

"It's all about accountability," my younger son, Chris, said. He is a manager with a nonprofit company.

"If something needs to be finished, stay to get the job done, even if it is 5:00 pm. Do this on your own without anyone asking you," he said.

Taking it one step further are employees who anticipate what will come next. They are prepared to jump on it, the definition of being proactive.

"It's all about exceeding expectations, what I can anticipate, and taking it a step above," a young professional said. "It's knowing that I am already on it when my boss mentions it."

Richard Boardman, associate dean for Development and Alumni Relations at Harvard Law School, told me about a study that identified top competencies of fund-raisers. Being proactive was number one.

"When you are a self-starter and have the right attitude, you can do anything," he stated.

Another way to exceed expectations is to offer to do more.

"Volunteering to take on tasks before being asked is pretty easy after being in a job for a few months and you see that work flow is predictable," said Ross Geisel, a database analyst with an international charitable organization.

Bosses notice this type of performance. And mediocre work gets noted as well.

> *Laziness comes through very quickly, so word gets out regarding who to avoid asking to help out.*
> **23-year-old professional**

"Employers are renting you for eight hours," Scott Wallace, with Anne Arundel Workforce Development Corporation, said. "They expect you to do the best job you can."

# SUMMARY

- Get everything done well, not only on time.
- Exceed expectations.
- Anticipate problems, and be ready to jump on them should they occur.

## What Attributes This Simple Way Demonstrates
- Responsibility
- Work Ethic

## Why Employers Want This
- It provides a sense of confidence that quality work will be produced.
- When work does not have to be examined in detail for possible errors, stress level will be diminished.
- They do not have to deal with a negative attitude.

# SIMPLE ACTION STEPS

Start Date:_____

1. On the job, if your boss is not pleased with your work, tell him or her that you will make the corrections promptly. How you redo the tasks will make an impression as well. To build your reputation as a responsible employee, demonstrate a positive attitude through your words and facial expressions instead of complaining about the work.
2. If you are in school, the next time you do not make the grade, be honest about your effort. Did you turn it in late? What could you have done to produce a quality product?

3. If you are not done with a task and a friend calls to go out, finish it before you leave, making certain it meets expectations. It is even better if it exceeds them.

Notes _____

_____

_____

_____

_____

_____

_____

_____

_____

_____

_____

_____

_____

_____

_____

_____

_____

_____

_____

_____

_____

# 9

# Simple Way #6
# Can You Hear Me Now?
# Good.

*Treat everyone as if he/she were the president
of the company calling.
It really doesn't matter who the person is.
The call must have the same sense of urgency.
This will give you a flawless reputation.*
Mary McMurtry, Southwest Airlines

About four times a year, I receive a postcard in the mail reminding me that the carpets in my home need to be cleaned. My husband and I have used the same carpet cleaning service for 10 years, so the postcards give me the nudge I need to make the call.

I recently contacted Gary Palmieri, franchisee of C & G Chem-Dry, and heard a recorded statement, "We check our voice mail messages regularly, and you will receive a return call in 30 minutes."

Sure enough, in about 10 minutes, the phone rang, and an appointment was booked. I was quite impressed by how quickly Gary returned my call. He actually did what he pledged he would do.

When Gary came to clean the rugs, I asked why he started that policy.

"I get tired of contacting service people who don't return my calls, so this was a way to treat my customers like I wanted to be treated myself," he said.

Apparently, many people feel as Gary does. More than 500,000 home-owners in 124 major cities have joined Angie's List, an online service that recommends favorite service companies. Their ad starts with, "Tired of Lousy Service?"

Gary's policy of promptly returning calls has led to repeat business being the bulk of his clientele. People know they can count on him.

How often do you get a return phone call so promptly? When you do, isn't it more of a surprise than an expectation? Add "pleasant" to surprise because, unfortunately, it seems to be increasingly rare these days.

Why is that? Maybe it is technology. Instant messaging is easier, but returning a phone call and e-mail as quickly as you can pay dividends because of how people then feel about you.

If you do this consistently and in a professional manner, people feel respected. They feel that they matter. I'm not talking about returning unsolicited sales calls. Rather, I'm referring to important calls from people requesting assistance or needing an answer. Maybe they want to do business with the company for whom you work.

This applies to e-mails, too. Everyone gets hundreds of unwanted messages, but you can scan them quickly and identify which ones are important.

Kaely Roe of Severna Perk described a time when an employee's failure to return Kaely's call cost the worker her job. The employee wanted to get her shift covered on a Saturday. It was the responsibility of the workers to make those arrangements. Kaely called repeatedly to make sure the shift was covered because this employee never got back in touch to confirm that she had found workers.

When Kaely had not heard from the employee by Thursday night, she decided to line up workers for the shift. Kaely finally heard from the employee on Friday night at 10:30. Her shift was Saturday at 7:30 am. When asked why she didn't call, the employee kept saying, "I don't know what to say." There was no remorse. The employee was let go.

You might have some friends who do not get back to you. If this happens a lot, you start to wonder if you can count on them. That's where reputation comes in. A person who returns phone calls and e-mails gets a reputation as someone who is considerate of others, is responsible, and, in the business arena, is efficient.

When you are on the job, this is key. Your boss may hear complimentary feedback about the prompt response. It is one more way to build the reputation you want.

# SUMMARY

- Determine which phone calls are important, and return them promptly.
- The same applies to e-mails.

## What Attributes This Simple Way Demonstrates
- Responsibility
- Respect

## Why Employers Want This
- It enhances the belief you are competent.
- Customers and clients love prompt return phone calls and e-mails.
- It demonstrates you are professional.

# SIMPLE ACTION STEPS

Start Date:_____

1. On the job, make returning business-related phone calls a priority when you get to work. If you cannot get back to the person with requested information immediately, leave a message to say when you can. People wonder when they do not hear back. If you eliminate that worry, people feel respected. Some business advice books will say that you should call within 24 to 48 hours. I believe that is too long. Make contact as soon as you can.
2. If you are in school, promptly return calls from professors, students, family, and friends. Get in the habit of following up. When people know they can count on you, your reputation benefits.
3. The same philosophy applies to e-mail. Send a reply in no more than 12 to 24 hours. If you can't answer a question right away, send an e-mail to explain why you can't. Make it concise and well-written. It is one more way to build your reputation.

Notes

# 10

# Simple Way #7
# Chew Pride Carefully
# Before Swallowing

*Everyone is going to make mistakes.*
*You just need to learn and grow in spite of them.*
Teresa Divers, Production Coordinator, Under Armour

One windy morning in Baltimore, Maryland, I visited Under Armour, originator of performance apparel for athletes, to talk with Jim Fulks and Teresa Divers. We spent a good deal of time talking about one of the hardest things to do, specifically, admit mistakes.

Fearing the unknown, people hate to own up to their mistakes. We see that repeatedly in the news. National figures, who would be so much better off if they would just come clean, don't. Instead, when it is clear to everyone that they are guilty as charged, they compound the problem with denials and excuses. If they just stepped to the plate early on, it would be over and forgotten.

The same is true in the workplace. Employees who admit to mistakes— while offering solutions—are viewed in a much more positive light than those who don't. People who do not blame others but accept responsibility exhibit the integrity an employer values.

Jim recalled an example of a costly mistake. Under Armour decided to make gloves for batters, manufacturing only a limited number for key accounts. Several salesmen sold them. There were soon orders for more than the initial production run. However, the person who could have alerted management to the problem deflected responsibility. When he saw all the orders coming in, he assumed the salespeople had inflated figures and did not say anything.

What would Under Armour do? Making another run for the additional 150,000 would be costly, but they decided that they did not have any other choice in order to fulfill customer expectations.

This act of omission cost the company in ways besides dollars. People lost respect for this person and started to check his numbers. This created suspicion that the whole system was off. Everybody checked—and rechecked—figures, and the sales, production, and manufacturing departments were not working well together. It was fixed, but it was at the cost of people, time, and respect.

"It goes to responsibility," Jim said. "I can't train people to take action when they see problems. The last thing any manager wants to hear is that you've seen a problem and done nothing. This is not taking responsibility."

But the fear of being criticized or chastised can prevent employees from admitting their mistakes.

"In general, people don't like to speak up," Teresa said. "No one wants to take the blame. They want to find someone else who made the mistake. And this can cause trust issues between and within departments."

Jim said the following about a person's lack of ability to own up to mistakes, "It takes three to six months to build trust in a business setting. It takes about two seconds to destroy it."

Admitting mistakes is one more component of responsibility. And your ability to take constructive criticism is equally important.

## Tip to Remember

Be sure to tell your boss about mistakes before he/she hears about them from someone else. Never let him or her be surprised.

# SUMMARY

- Admit your mistakes.
- Think about how to solve the problem. Be ready to learn from constructive criticism.

## What Attributes This Simple Way Demonstrates
- Responsibility
- Integrity/Honesty

## Why Employers Want This
- They feel reassured that their decision to hire you was sound.
- They can trust you to alert them when problems arise and take responsibility.
- They can depend on you to provide solutions.

# SIMPLE ACTION STEPS

**Start Date:**_____

1. Be on the lookout for mistakes you make. When you do, think first about how to remedy it. What can you do to fix the problem?
2. If the mistake is one that impacts other people, take this solution to the appropriate person at work, in a group, or within your family. If it influences other people, make certain that you do not wait too long to admit the mistake.
3. Practice stating solutions in a calm manner. Admit the mistake. Apologize as appropriate, but keep your emotions in check.

Notes_____

_____

_____

_____

_____

_____

_____

_____

_____

_____

_____

_____

_____

_____

_____

_____

# 11

# Simple Way #8
# Uh...You're Welcome

*It's the simple things you do. People love to feel appreciated.*
Ryan Elkins, Financial Advisor, Ameriprise Financial

The power of expressing appreciation is amazing. Ryan Elkins, a financial advisor in his twenties, has perfected this simple way. Whether it is with his clients or colleagues, Ryan understands the impact of saying thank you.

"When you have a reputation for being appreciative, you stand out," Ryan noted. "More people want to help you, and they say good things about you. Clients send new referrals your way, too."

Showing appreciation is a company culture at Ameriprise. Every Monday, the staff is given time to publicly say thank you to coworkers.

"We spend so much time together that we are like a second family," Ryan said.

Employees at Ameriprise will send flowers to each other in gratitude for help they have received. Ryan plans unusual thank-you outings for clients, such as a day at the spa or a cooking class at a historic inn. He also sends them a special glass each time he receives a new client. Ryan told me that people look forward to collecting a set of six glasses.

Consistently saying thank you demonstrates your respect for others. Your boss sees that you know what to say. He can be reassured that you will extend gratitude to customers or clients.

As a little kid, your parents probably taught you to say thank you. Then, somewhere along the way, being too busy or day-to-day activities consumed your attention. Writing a thank-you note was on your "To Do" list, but you thought, "Hey, they know I liked the gift or appreciated what they did for me." Saying thanks gets lost in the pile.

Later on, this may spill over into the workplace. A fellow employee may pick up the slack for you, and you will fail to thank him. A customer may make a purchase, and you say nothing.

As Ryan knows so well, do not wait to say thank you.

> Expressing your appreciation before you even get the job will be recognized. Employers say that receiving a thank-you letter from one of the applicants following an interview can make the difference, both being equal.

# SUMMARY

Say thank you every day.

## What Attribute This Simple Way Demonstrates
- Respect

## Why Employers Want This
- It makes the company look good.
- Customers and clients comment about appreciation being shown to them.
- It shows good manners.

# SIMPLE ACTION STEPS

Start Date:_____

1. Buy some thank-you note cards to have available.
2. Think about the people who have helped you in the past month. Write at least one thank-you letter to a coworker, professor, friend, or mentor. This builds your reputation as being thoughtful. People are happy to help others who are appreciative.
3. Each time you receive a gift, favor, or help, immediately thank the person, and then write a handwritten note.

Notes_____

_____
_____
_____
_____
_____
_____
_____
_____
_____
_____
_____
_____
_____
_____
_____
_____
_____
_____

# 12

# Simple Way #9
# 14AA41

*It's not just about doing my job.*
*It's about doing what is needed to be done*
*to make Southwest successful.*
Mary McMurtry, Southwest Airlines

"It's part of our culture," Mary explained. "Every group is a team, regardless of what job you have. There is no way one person can be an island."

Mary McMurtry was talking about the importance of helping others on the job and the impact not helping each other can have on the profitability of the company. "One for all and all for one," or 14AA41, is a philosophy Southwest employees practice every day at work.

"Airplanes don't make any money sitting on the ground," Mary said. "There is a 25-minute download and upload time. Luggage needs to be taken off and new bags need to be put on. In addition, 135 people leave the plane, and new passengers then come on board during this 25-minute time frame. This is an industry record."

"It's not uncommon to see pilots helping the ramp agents with mail and luggage if the flight is running late," Mary said. "Flight attendants help the operation agents. When there is no more bin space, flight attendants get bag tags and put them on."

This sense of helping others is taken a step further with the Southwest Airlines Employee Catastrophic Fund, which employees solely support. When employees are in crisis, they can apply for assistance. Approximately $2 million has been given to employees.

Mary recalled an example of extraordinary compassion shown to a ramp supervisor whose young wife was ill and then died. The employee was devastated. When he needed more than the allotted four days, coworkers volunteered to pick up his work shift till he was ready to come back to work.

"It is so ingrained in us to help," she said.

Consider the opposite example of an employee, who says, "Hey, I did my 50 calls. That's it. I'm going home."

Never mind that this employee's coworkers are struggling to meet the company's quota. That does not matter to her.

This type of worker is every employer's nightmare. She does not have the mentality of a team. She does not care that fellow workers need her help. She thinks it is time to go home and she has done her share.

Bosses care more about the prosperity of the company, not your personal convenience or success. Everybody is responsible for the bottom line—whether you are in sales or not. Being a team player and pitching in when needed demonstrates to others that you care about the organization's health and fellow workers.

In addition to helping out, there are other ways you will be able to assist others, for example, offering to show a new employee the way it is done around the company or working to solve a problem.

Best yet are the employees who do not have to be asked to help out. That is how you really build your reputation and move ahead.

# SUMMARY

- Practice the 14AA41 philosophy: "One for all and all for one."
- Offer to help…before you are asked.
- Pitch in, even when your part is done.

## What Attribute This Simple Way Demonstrates
- Leadership

## Why Employers Want This
- It demonstrates you care about the company.
- It shows you are an asset to the organization.
- It reinforces the belief that you are a person of character.

# SIMPLE ACTION STEPS

Start Date:_____

1. On the job, watch for opportunities to help coworkers. Focus on this simple way until you do not have to think about helping others. You just automatically offer.
2. If you are in school and see a fellow student struggling with an assignment, offer to answer questions.
3. Volunteer in the community as often as you can. Be involved in the groups you join. If time is an issue, pick a Saturday to support a worthy cause.

Notes_____

_____

_____

_____

_____

_____

_____

_____

_____

_____

_____

_____

_____

_____

_____

_____

_____

_____

_____

_____

_____

_____

_____

_____

_____

_____

_____

_____

_____

# 13

# Simple Way #10
# What's Your Problem?

*Do you know I've been with the store over eight years
and I'm still only part-time?*
Jason, Grocery Store Clerk

Jason (not his real name) was helping me load groceries into my car. He was telling me how unhappy he was with his work situation. In fact, I heard the same thing every time I saw him. This time, he had some other news.

"Our house is for sale," Jason said. "We're going to move to Pennsylvania and get a fresh start."

Jason is a young man in his twenties. He lives with his parents, and I have talked with him for more than eight years. At first, I would see him in the parking lot area. He later moved into the store, but he only occasionally worked as a cashier.

I have never heard a positive comment from him. I'm sure this is not lost on his supervisor. Why isn't he full-time? Could his constant complaining be the reason?

Complaining affects customers as well. I was put in an awkward situation by employees at a greeting card store. While I browsed through cards in the back aisle, two store clerks started talking about other customers.

"She comes in here all the time," the first clerk said, referring to a woman who had just left the store. "She reminds me why I wish they (customers) would all stay home. They talk so much. I can never get my work done."

Then the clerk paused and said, "Is anybody else in here?"

Not knowing what to do, I quietly walked along the back row to the other side of the store. The clerks continued to complain about their workload until another customer came in.

What type of impression did I have about this store? It was certainly not a positive one, and I relayed my experience to several friends and family members.

People, particularly bosses, get tired of complainers. On the job, if you complain about work assignments or tasks that are not in your job description, your employer will not be pleased.

If you gripe about your boss to fellow workers or if you go over the head of your immediate supervisor to those higher up the company ladder, your reputation will greatly suffer because you will be branded as disloyal.

A supervisor spoke candidly about an employee who has the reputation for being "the complainer."

"She's good in terms of performance because of her raw talent," the supervisor said. "But we can't pay attention to other workers who need and want development because we're always managing her reactions."

One afternoon this employee stopped her supervisor and other managers in the hallway to express her displeasure.

"I really don't like this new idea," she said. When told it was not an idea but rather a change in policy, she responded with, "Well, nobody else likes this idea either."

What future does this employee have at the company?

"She is given no responsibility, and will never be a manager," the supervisor said. "With her attitude, we can't afford to have her represent us. I often wonder if she is the bad apple that could spoil the bunch."

Chronic complainers, like this employee, the card store clerks, and Jason, believe they are not to blame for their troubles. They are focused outward causing bosses to be exasperated. One manager said, "Does everything have to be a problem?"

When you feel the need to complain, do so outside the work environment with only trusted friends … or your dog.

# SUMMARY

- Choose when and where to complain.
- Do not bring complaints about personal life to work.
- Do not complain about fellow workers or go over the head of your immediate boss.

## What Attribute This Simple Way Demonstrates
- Respect

## Why Employers Don't Want This
- Complaining gets very tiring and annoying.
- It takes time away from productive work to deal with it.
- It is unprofessional.

# SIMPLE ACTION STEPS

**Start Date:**_____

1.  Count the number of times you complain about anything in a day. Do this for one week.
2.  Once you see how often you complain, confine your rants to a specified time each day, preferably by yourself, away from your job, or people who are not very close and trusted friends.

Notes_____

_____

_____

_____

_____

_____

_____

_____

_____

_____

_____

_____

_____

_____

_____

_____

_____

_____

_____

_____

# 14

# Simple Way #11
# Staying in Front
# of the Curve

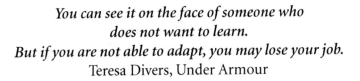

*You can see it on the face of someone who*
*does not want to learn.*
*But if you are not able to adapt, you may lose your job.*
Teresa Divers, Under Armour

"If you are not open to learning, it stunts your growth," Teresa told me. "Maybe you are not the perfect fit for something you are asked to do. But if you protest that you don't have the skills or don't know how to do something, you'll never get the challenging opportunities that will help your career move forward."

How do you develop the ability to jump on opportunities, even when you wonder if you have the necessary skills? One simple way is to take a course that does not relate to your field of interest. Trying something new and out of your comfort zone is a great exercise. Continuing to expand your mind and skill set is something employers highly value. They will expect this behavior throughout your career. It also gets you in the mindset that, in order to stay competitive, lifelong learning is the only option.

Lifelong learning is a core belief held at colleges across the country. This is certainly the case at Anne Arundel Community College, chosen in 2001 as community college of the year by the National Alliance of Business.

Martha Smith, PhD, is president of Anne Arundel Community College. She encourages students to get in the habit of asking questions.

"This is the age of the knowledge worker," she said. "To be successful, you need to be inquisitive about your work and clear about the expectations of the position rather than assuming what is expected. Asking the right questions and seeking the training or professional development you need will be your responsibility."

> Dr. Smith encourages students to ask themselves the question, "What will I need to know tomorrow that I don't know today?"

On the job, the way you have done particular tasks may abruptly change when the company's direction shifts. You will be required to be flexible and possibly master a new skill quickly. That is where embracing learning will serve you well.

"Be teachable," my daughter-in-law, Jenny, said. Jenny, a former high school teacher, is now the director of enrollment at Laureate Education. "Too often we hear the excuse train. Be honest about what you are good at, but be open to learning new skills," she said.

Lifelong learning helps you discover new ways of doing things. The new skills you acquire may show you how to solve a problem. You can then demonstrate to superiors that you have the necessary skills to tackle your job well.

# SUMMARY

- To get in the habit of learning things new to you, take a course in a subject outside your comfort zone.
- To advance in your career, lifelong learning is a given.
- Practice asking good questions.

## What Attribute This Simple Way Demonstrates
- Adaptability

## Why Employers Want This
- It demonstrates your flexibility, adaptability, and openness to change.
- It shows your ability to acquire new skills that may be needed to move in a new direction.
- You may learn solutions to problems.

# SIMPLE ACTION STEPS

Start Date:_____

1. Finish reading this book, and practice the **12 Simple Ways.**
2. Identify areas where you are weak, and seek out courses or training you can take.
3. Ask people questions about your area of interest to learn what skills they have needed. Refer to chapter 16 for help with talking with people and networking.

Notes _____

# 15

# Simple Way #12
# No, Really—Shut Up!

*We have two ears and one mouth so that we can
listen twice as much as we speak.*
Epictetus (c. 55–c. 135),
Greek Stoic Philosopher

How many times have you wondered if the person you were talking to really heard what you said? Or was that person so busy preparing what to say next that you were totally tuned out? Maybe you've done it yourself. I know I have.

This sometimes comes from being excited about a particular topic. Consequently, it is hard to just stop and listen. On the job, you may miss some vital instructions or other information if you interrupt to make a point or share your great idea. If you are new, you risk appearing naïve. Coworkers may think you are just trying to impress the boss.

Employers value workers who have the ability to recommend solutions to problems, but there is also a caveat to mention. As a new employee, your ideas may not be well received. In reality, other workers do not know you or your reputation. Will you suggest an idea and not follow through? Can they count on you? You must earn credibility first, and you do that by genuinely listening and learning.

Former UN Secretary General Kofi Annan made an observation that I heard quoted at a college commencement, "Never walk into an environment and assume that you understand it better than the people who live there."

You do not want to go charging into a new job and push your idea without understanding the work environment, even if you believe it will solve a problem. People might think you just do not get it. They might believe you are a know-it–all or naïve. They might think you haven't taken the time to get to know the company culture of "how we do things around here."

I made that mistake in a job I had. After being in the position for three months, I was certain I had a great idea for a new program. But I had not done enough research to understand that the idea was impractical and would never be accepted. I submitted it. Of course, it was rejected right away. I ignored this simple way by not listening and learning first.

Jennifer Stillings, president of worldAWAKE and former Navy pilot of 40 combat missions, recalled advice she heard before she began flying.

It was, "Be quiet. Ask the people who have more experience for their advice."

"I found this to be invaluable," Jennifer said. "I realized that my technical knowledge was there, and what I needed were the insights beyond what it 'said in the book.' By keeping my mouth shut— even when I thought I had 'the' answer for a problem—I gained the confidence and respect of others because I acknowledged the wisdom coming my way."

Jennifer said that when you start out in any organization, you are not the expert.

"Before you offer solutions or criticisms, you need to learn how things are done in your new work environment," she noted. "Listening and learning before you speak are so important for both your professional development and your working relationships. This advice helped me establish a sound reputation within the first three to six months."

Always think of creative ideas. Just be sure you know "how we do things around here" before you propose them. Stop. Listen first. Maybe what the person is saying will change what you suggest.

# SUMMARY

- Listen first. Hear what the other person says before you speak.
- Do not interrupt.

## What Attribute This Simple Way Demonstrates
- Respect

## Why Employers Want This
- It demonstrates you are patient and thoughtful.
- It shows you will not waste time asking for information to be repeated.
- It shows respect for your boss and coworkers.

# SIMPLE ACTION STEPS

Start Date:_____

1. Ask a friend to tell you each time you interrupt the conversation. Observe when you finish the sentence for someone else.

2. In a small group setting with friends, coworkers, or students, let the other person finish speaking before you respond. This may take several conversations before you can break the habit of interrupting someone else.

Notes_____

_____

_____

_____

_____

_____

_____

_____

_____

_____

_____

_____

_____

_____

_____

_____

_____

_____

_____

_____

_____

# 16

# Let's Meet in Real Life

*First, you have to be visible in the community. You have to get out there and connect with people. It's not called net-sitting or net-eating. It's called networking. You have to work at it.*
Ivan Misner, PhD, Founder & Chairman,
Business Networking International

If you are graduating this year or have a few more to go, the thought of having to find a job is probably on your mind. As you near graduation, it seems that everyone is asking ad nauseam, "What do you want to do?"

When asked so often, this question can create pressure or even be annoying because you may not know the answer yet. But you hear yourself saying, "I have to find a job. I wonder how to go about it. Whom should I talk to? What am I supposed to say to them?"

Maybe you are out of school and in the midst of looking for a job. During this search, you will often need to talk to people you do not know. This can produce anxiety, particularly if you are an introvert. "What will we talk about? Will they even listen to me?" you think.

It may be that you are on the job right now and stuck in neutral. How can you move your career forward? By networking, and in addition to the **12 Simple Ways,** networking know-how is the most useful skill you can learn at any stage of your career.

What is networking exactly? According to Anne Baber and Lynne Waymon, networking experts, it is teaching people who you are and providing information about your character and competence, the building blocks of a great reputation.

Some people believe it is just seeing what you can get from others. This is not true. Instead, networking must be mutually beneficial. Spend a lot of time learning about other people. If you are just graduating, do not assume you have nothing to give. You might know about a computer program shortcut or a great new book you can recommend.

Anne and Lynne run a nationwide training company called Contacts Count and have written *Make Your Contacts Count.* They gave me some tips that you can practice:

## Concentrate on Names

How often have you been introduced and then forgot the name seconds later? We rush right through the name to get to the "good stuff" in the conversation, not realizing that the name is the good stuff, according to Lynne and Anne.

"People spend about six seconds exchanging names," Lynne said. "You can do a lot in six seconds, but one thing you can't do is teach someone your name and learn hers."

*I wish I had made a point to remember names while I was an undergrad. There were so many times when I forgot the name of the person I was talking to almost immediately. I think you have an advantage if you know how to remember names, particularly in the work world.*

**Laura, graduate student**

There are specific techniques you can use to master the name exchange.

To learn someone's name:
- **Repeat it.** If the other person says his or her name first, repeat the first name in your greeting. Say, "Hi, Jim. It's good to meet you."
- **Ask about it.** You might ask about the spelling. "Do you spell your name with a 'c' or a 'k'?"
- **Ask for the last name separately.** Say, "Tell me your last name again."

To teach your name:
- **Give your first name twice.** Say, "I'm Julie. Julie Warner."
- **Say both your names clearly and distinctly.** Do not run them together.
- **Give a tip for people to remember your name.** Say, "It's Dell, like the computer."

## What Do You Want To Do?

How you answer this question determines whether the conversation moves forward or just limps along.

First, Anne suggested answers to definitely avoid. Do not say:
- "I'll do anything."
- The title of the job you want
- Your major if you are in school ("I'm an English major.")
- Your industry ("I'm looking for something in health care.")
- Limiting your occupation ("I'm looking for a position in employee communications.")

The problem with these answers is that they are either too broad or too narrow. People can't get a clear picture of what you're looking for. Instead, say what you want someone to remember about you and a quick example that brings your job hunt to life.

If you are still in school, you could say, for example, "I've just designed a marketing program for a law firm as a final project in one of my classes. As part of my research, I interviewed several marketing directors. I'd be very interested in any job that involved publicity for an organization."

People can visualize this type of answer and have a better sense of what you are looking for.

## Deciding What to Talk About

Before you talk with people, think about things you can share. Contacts Count calls this "being prepared to be spontaneous." It could be a resource, tips, shortcuts, or something you are enthusiastic about.

Think about things you want to find, learn, or connect with. When someone asks if anything is new, have something in mind, such as, "I've spent a lot of time researching various organizations on the Internet. Do you know anybody who designs Web sites?"

## Ask for Advice, Not a Job or Job Lead

People love to give advice. Instead of directly asking for a job, particularly when they do not know you, seek advice. As the relationship grows, this may lead to your hearing about a job.

## Getting Started

To build your network from scratch, try these ideas from Contacts Count:

- If you do not have a business card, get a "career" or "networking" card. Include your name, address, and phone number as well as a few words about what you do. It could be "chemical engineer" or "graphic design for newsletters, brochures, and annual reports."
- Plug into your family's network. They can introduce you to their networking contacts.
- Contact the people you already know. These include former employers, professors, college alumni, fraternity/ sorority alumni, church members, neighbors, and relatives.
- Ask everyone two things: advice on how to find the job you want and names of people they know whom you

should contact. Ask your contacts to call those people on your behalf. Then you do not need to send a résumé to someone who has never heard of you.

- Request feedback about your résumé. Be sure to include a postage paid envelope so the person you've asked can send it back to you at no cost. Once you receive their comments, be sure to send a thank-you note.

- Join organizations related to your field of interest, such as a professional association. Then be sure to volunteer to help so you become visible to the other members.

Another benefit of networking is the improvement of your communication skills, which we have seen as one of the top priorities of employers.

A very interesting example of the power of networking happened to me a couple years ago. Serving as an interim director, I was helping with the search for the new executive. We had two finalists, both of whom were highly qualified.

A person we all knew and highly regarded contacted the search committee. She had a recommendation for the position. Because we were in the final stages of the job search, there was a reluctance to extend the process. However, since this was a reputable word of mouth referral, we interviewed the woman. She was outstanding. She got the job.

## A Tip for College Students

*Freshman year is the best time to go to networking and career events because there is no pressure. Once it matters (junior/ senior years), you have the routine down, and you are familiar with the job application process. Network with alumni and other administrators on campus. Stay positive, and don't think you have to map out your entire career now.*

23-year-old professional

Notes_____

_____

_____

_____

_____

_____

_____

_____

_____

_____

_____

_____

_____

_____

_____

_____

_____

_____

_____

_____

_____

_____

_____

_____

_____

# 17

# To Whom it May Concern

*What matters to prospective employers?*
*I think it is your ability to present yourself professionally,*
*knowing the background of the company and the position before*
*coming in, showing confidence, having the ability to sell yourself,*
*and feeling comfortable highlighting your strengths.*
Stacey Koons, Enrollment Manager,
Laureate Education

Most people think, "How will I find a job?" In fact, the majority of questions I heard in focus groups related to this concern.

Many of the attributes discussed in this book will be useful during the job interview. Nancy Fink, assistant director of the Professional Out-placement Assistance Center with the Maryland Department of Labor, Licensing, and Regulation, counsels job seekers to answer questions in a way that demonstrates the qualities employers want.

"Job candidates may write on their résumés that they are dependable and have integrity," Nancy said. "But those are intangible traits. You need to define them with stories or examples that show employers they can count on you to get the work done on time and under budget. These are the things employers care about."

When you practice the 12 Simple Ways, you will have plenty of examples. You can talk about your role in a successful team project, or how you helped past or current employers. You will have the meaningful references from former supervisors or professors who observed your work ethic. Through your efforts, your reputation for being a hard worker is being established.

Once you have determined the type of job you'd like, you are ready to concentrate on the job search. Several comprehensive books and Web sites about this process are available. Check the Appendix for some of the really good ones.

The employers I interviewed had some quick and important tips to assist your search as well.

## Interview Attire
If you are uncertain about what to wear, be sure to overdress rather than underdress.

## Errors on Résumés
One error could matter. You cannot get around making sure there are no mistakes. Proof it several times before giving it to others. They can then catch mistakes you might have missed.

## Value of Internships
If you are still in school, a great place to begin building your reputation is in an internship. They are often available during the summer, both paid and unpaid. Because employers like to see relevant work experience, it is worth seeking out internships during the summers of your sophomore and junior years. While they may not pay, they are a perfect place to practice the **12 Simple Ways**. Your boss will notice if you consistently demonstrate to people that they can count on you.

You may also be able to secure an impressive recommendation letter from the internship experience, or even receive a job lead.

> *Not only did my first internship supervisor give me a recommendation, he hired me full-time after I graduated from college. When I was a summer intern, I went above and beyond my responsibilities, and I took the time to learn about the company and introduce myself in all departments.*
> Meghan Kwasniak, Enrollment Manager
> Laureate Education

For detailed information about internships, check the resources in the Appendix.

Simply put, you need them.

## Gaps of Inactivity

Employers do not like to see periods of inactivity. In addition to internships and other work experience, volunteer during times of unemployment. Show your responsibility in this way.

## Extracurricular Activities

With little work experience, students wonder if joining on-campus clubs will carry the same weight. According to several career counselors with whom I spoke, employers look for leadership roles rather than extensive involvement in a number of clubs. Find a club, school, or community project in your area of interest, and seek leadership opportunities.

## References

Jenny Hall is constantly in the hiring mode at Laureate Education. She had a few words to say about references. "Be sure to pick your references wisely. Choose people who are well-spoken," she advised. "This does not necessarily mean a person's title."

Employers will check with references. If they do not communicate well, questions about your credibility or reputation may be the result, even if they praise you.

"You'll sometimes want to avoid people with impressive titles just because they do not speak well," Jenny said.

## Several Interviews at One Company

"Be prepared to go through as many as five interviews," Sallie Hays with the Maryland Governor's Workforce Investment Board said. "The first interview is generally a telephone screening interview. Subsequent interviews may be one-on-one or with a panel. Interviewers are looking for someone with the personality and enthusiasm to fit in with the company, as well as having the required technical skills."

## Thank-You Letters

You have read about the impact that appreciation can have on the job. The same holds true for an interview. If you demonstrate appreciation and the other candidate does not, you may have the edge if everything appears to be equal.

Writing both a brief e-mail expressing thanks and a note or letter is best. Be sure to include that you are very interested in the position and want to work for the company or organization. Stress the qualifications you possess that closely match what they are looking for as well as skills you may have forgotten to mention during the interview.

Writing a thank-you letter demonstrates you understand the importance of good manners.

## Determining What the Company Needs

Perhaps one of the worst interviews I ever had was for a job where my own "agenda" got in the way. I applied for a position and was certain that my abilities would be perfect for the job. However, I wanted to make sure the leadership style practiced in my current work situation was not happening in this new company.

My questions to them were too strong. I used examples that were completely irrelevant. My emotions simply defeated me. I did not get the job. Based on my poor interview, I shouldn't have.

It is important to research the company you are applying to. What do they need? How can your skills help them? It is all about how you can help them.

## Interview Attitude

"Treat every interview with respect. Regardless of how casual the company is, it is still an interview," Mary McMurtry said. "Speak in complete sentences. If you are applying for an adult job, speak like an adult."

In her experience, job candidates have done the research on a company, but many lose their personality in the interview.

"People hire human beings. Let them see what you are all about."

## Networking—Once Again

According to Meghan Kwasniak, "Don't just leave everyone behind once you leave school. Be sure to stay in touch with professors and alumni."

You never know when those connections might help you.

## The Role of Reputation

"It's the lynchpin," Mary McMurtry said. "Smart hiring managers in companies—small or large—will try to find out about job candidates by calling previous employers. You want to hear them say, 'We should clone that guy.' Your reputation needs to be sterling to go anywhere. If not, it will catch up with you."

*There are many different qualities that employers look for. When hiring entry-level employees, I think they want someone who is dependable and has the drive to do well. You can see in someone's attitude if he or she is the type of person who will do whatever it takes. That is what they want.*

Meghan Kwasniak

Notes _____

_____

_____

_____

_____

_____

_____

_____

_____

_____

_____

_____

_____

_____

_____

_____

_____

_____

_____

_____

_____

# 18

# Beyond the 12 Simple Ways: What Twentysomethings and Employers Said Really Matters

In addition to the **12 Simple Ways,** being aware of other workplace realities will help you move ahead. The following brief tips have been broken down into the major attribute categories.

## Positive Attitude

*An "Attitude" Can Really Hurt You*
One supervisor commented about an attitude that is sometimes displayed by new employees. "They have given me the feeling that they are doing me a favor, like they are owed a job," she said. "That's frightening to think about. They need to realize the world doesn't revolve around them."

This kind of behavior can really doom you. Instead, demonstrate you can be trusted every day.

"It's learning how to start at the bottom," employees I interviewed said. "Or like climbing back up the totem pole."

*It's Okay to Have Fun*
A sense of humor is a wonderful attribute to bring to the workplace.

Kaely Roe told me about a male employee who wore the apron of a female employee named Amy when he was training on the job. Amy had designed the apron, and it had princess kittens on it. The customers loved it and kidded him about wearing Amy's apron.

"I knew he was someone who would fit in right away," Kaely said. "He simply made others laugh and have fun."

"Let them see your personality and laugh at yourself," Mary McMurtry said. "Work shouldn't be a four-letter word."

# Professionalism

*Slang*
"We would be afraid to ask some people to do a presentation to upper management," Chris Hall mentioned. "They might use words such as, 'I was … like … you know,' uh, yeah, or other slang. These people are unable to differentiate between who is in the room."

Next to dress, almost nothing forms a negative impression faster than improper words coming from your own mouth. This could be using bad grammar (for example, "I can't get no…") or slang before you know if it is acceptable in your workplace.

"The reality is that you will not see opportunities coming your way if you do not speak well," Chris said.

*Use Capitals in E-mails*
Written communication is important, too.

Laureate Education managers told me proper writing is often too casual, particularly in e-mails. "Don't abbreviate, be too informal, or forget to use capitals," they stressed. "Using 'i' instead of 'I' is annoying."

Just as you take great care to eliminate all mistakes in your résumé, accuracy in all writing in the workplace should be a top priority.

### Use Print, Not Cursive

One of the biggest wastes of time is trying to read someone's scribble. Many people take pride in a signature that no one can read. When you ensure a person can actually make out each letter, it is a subtle way to build a reputation.

### Pay Attention to Details

Kate Boardman, a recent college graduate, talked about how not being careful with the smallest details can disrupt the entire office.

"If you spell a client's name wrong, it can affect the whole office," she said. "I didn't realize I would need to pay so much attention to the little details."

### Use Proper Etiquette

Whether you are in an interview or meeting, you need to know how to act. Rachel Bandarenko, a business etiquette consultant, recommends three habits you can cultivate that will be useful in the workplace.

1.  Learn proper dining etiquette. In the work world, people notice when you do not follow the rules of etiquette. For example, you never should order alcohol on a job interview.

    Rachel recommends a small book you can keep in your pocket or purse. It has everything you need to know about dining etiquette. It is called *The Little Book of Etiquette* by Dorothea Johnson (Philadelphia: Running Press Miniature Edition, 1997).

2.  Send a handwritten thank-you note within 24 hours to a person who has helped you or has taken you out to eat. E-mail is okay and will slightly get you off the hook. But that is not extraordinary, and it won't set you apart. A handwritten note will.

3. Take any opportunity to engage in public speaking. The more you practice, the easier it gets. This helps you on the job interview, in networking, and on the job when you are talking with clients or coworkers.

Good manners and etiquette are essential because employers expect these qualities in people at all levels in the company.

### How You Sit Can Affect Your Boss

"I was a hard worker in college," a 25-year-old professional said. "But the supervisor at my first job didn't like the way I sat or dressed. She automatically assumed I was screwing around. She thought I was a slacker."

Something as basic as how you sit can have a profound impact. The young professional above did not realize that her appearance and the way she sat would cause her supervisor to perceive her as a slacker. Perception was the key. It had nothing to do with reality. However, to the employer, it was the truth.

### Keep Your Cool

One of the quickest ways to inspire doubt is to lose your cool. This could be a flash of anger, crying, or inappropriate laughter.

I remember an instance when the director of a nonprofit organization cried out of frustration at a board of directors meeting. This quickly changed the mood in the room, but, more importantly, the display of emotions affected all who were there.

This director later applied for another job in the community. Some of the same people on the board were part of the search committee for this new position. Consequently, she did not get the job.

You need to be in control of your emotions. Impressions stick. Even when faced with challenging situations, stay even and unflappable.

# Responsibility

*Work Outside Your Job Description*

How many people enjoy filing, copying, or grunt work? Probably not that many. If you have or will get your college degree, you may believe these jobs should be someone else's responsibility.

Laureate Education managers said you have to get a grip on what a bachelor's degree really means. "People blow up the significance of it as the end all," managers said. "They expect to find a fabulous job and great money right out of school."

"Your degree doesn't necessarily mean you'll be successful," a group of young professionals in New York City also told me. "It may get you your first job, but, after that, employers care more about things like determination and dependability."

In reality, you will be asked to do all sorts of things not in your job description even if you have been with the company for some time. It is all about what is best for the company.

You may be assigned more projects than you can handle at the same time. It is your responsibility to let your boss know that while you are happy to do a new task, you need to determine if the assignment has priority over your current work.

> *It is important not to assume that you are too good or too smart for the assignment you are given. If you don't take it seriously, you can never be expected to be given a more important assignment.*
> **23-year-old professional**

Jenny Hall talked about the reality of the workplace. "There is always something to do. Nothing is below you. You can't say, 'It's not my job.'

It's all our jobs." She also advised, "Don't complain if you are given copying to do or something you feel is outside your job description. If you do it cheerfully, people will be pleasantly surprised."

This is one more way to build a solid reputation.

> *When I'm not putting in the extra mile, my employees don't either. It's always important, no matter what your position, to show people energy and the desire to succeed.*
>
> Kaely Roe

## Work Ethic

*Time Management Tip while You are Still in School*
Scott Wallace said the best thing he ever did was take an on-campus job. "They knew I was a student first. They looked out for me. I could take time off the job to study because they knew I was a student first. But it also taught me time management. As a student you think, 'I can do that tomorrow,' but that is not the case when you work. You have to structure your time. I worked three days a week. I knew I had to get assignments done and play on the other days. It's a structure thing."

## Integrity/Honesty

*Living a Life with Integrity*
"It's all about acting to your beliefs when no one else knows or is looking," Carl Nanney said.

Carl told me about a particular employee who had found a substantial amount of money in a car he was repairing. This employee could have pocketed the money. Instead, he brought it to the company office to return to the owner.

"No one would have known," Carl said. "He acted with integrity."

That employee instantly had Carl's attention and recognition because he lived his values ... even when no one was looking.

*Don't Steal Your Employer's Time*
With advances in technology, the lure of the Internet can be overwhelming.

"I'll just check a couple sites and send a few e-mails before I start work. It won't take a second," you say.

After you have started, you might remember a great joke you want to pass along to friends or need to order a gift for your brother. Employers, however, view these few minutes as stolen time. They believe this time should be devoted to work.

Resisting the urge to steal time can be challenging, particularly when the boss is gone or you finish something early. But this time theft costs your employer in productivity and affects the bottom line.

*A Few More Integrity Issues*
A few more ways to show integrity include acknowledging your coworkers when they do something well, not stealing other people's ideas, and not lying to cover mistakes or missed deadlines.

# Respect

*Carefully Monitor Gossiping*
"I was surprised to see how catty some people can be," a young professional in her first job said.

Talking about colleagues in a negative way, or gossiping, is very damaging to you. You gain the reputation as a gossip. And there is no getting around the fact that, if you talk about others, they will talk about you.

> *To speak ill of others is a dishonest way of praising ourselves.*
> Will Durant (1885–1981),
> American philosopher, historian, and writer

But it is also a reality that you will gain a different kind of reputation if you are judgmental about others gossiping. Simply make it a practice to not repeat what you hear.

### Be a Leader and a Follower

In most books about qualities desired by employers, there will be a section about leadership traits.

However, before you concentrate on showing what an effective leader you can be, you will need to show your supervisor that you can follow.

My older son, Geoff, is chief of the Pavement & Geotechnical Division, Office of Materials Technology with the Maryland State Highway Administration. He told me about two employees whose personal behaviors determined their futures.

"When Frank (not his real name) was assigned to my team, I didn't know what kind of employee he was, but I had heard that he was sour and not a very good teammate. With George (not his real name), I had only heard that he was a 'good guy.' Since both Frank and George were alleged to have similar capabilities, they were given comparable assignments and responsibilities.

"Despite having few years of experience, Frank quickly showed that he could be counted on to do the job, no matter what it was. He took the initiative to get things done right and on time. If he was stuck or had a question, Frank was not afraid to ask for help. He listened and acted upon any critique, and he used that to improve his work. Frank was always courteous and professional. He ultimately made me confident that he could fill in for me when needed, without my worrying if he would do a good job.

"George, on the other hand, had a different outlook. Sure, he was a good guy, but just in terms of politeness. His inability at times to do what was asked of him, to follow the simplest of directions, was mind-numbing. Any critique was viewed as a personal attack because he'd say, 'I've been doing this for years.' George's lack of productivity constantly held up the rest of the team, and others had to cover for him. Due to some staffing shortages, he requested—and was given—an opportunity to hold a leadership position in an acting capacity. He failed miserably. The employees he supervised nearly rebelled, and complaints from clients rolled in. There was no way I could count on him. The thought of him interacting with clients made me cringe.

"Frank has proven that he can follow. By being able to do that, he has established that he can be counted on. Thus, he has proven that he can lead. Consequently, he is viewed as a leader by most of the employees within our division, whether or not he has an official position. He has been given leadership responsibilities and, with that, the freedom and ability to set his work agenda and garner respect from his peers and supervisors. For Frank, the sky is the limit. He understands that, if you do good work, good things will happen.

"George believes—and has stated on many occasions—that he deserves to be made a leader because of his several years of experience. However, his body of work has most definitely proven otherwise. Even when given a temporary leadership role, he could not be counted on. As such, when it came time to officially fill the leadership position, he was not offered the job."

First, demonstrate that you can follow directions, listen well, work in a team setting, and meet deadlines. Once your boss and coworkers have confidence you can deliver, you can highlight your leadership abilities.

# Leadership

*Help Supervisors See Your Motivation*
There are things you can do to enhance your ability to move forward. You can have goals. You can let your boss know you are committed and want to move up in the organization.

To demonstrate this, keep your employer informed about what you accomplish, for example, how you identified and then solved a problem. Let your boss know when something you have done was innovative or improved the bottom line.

Simply write a brief account of your activities on a regular basis. It can be just a few paragraphs. Include requests for professional development or other assistance. It shows you are committed and confident.

In many of my jobs, I have sent a monthly account of things I accomplished. No one asked me to do that. I wanted my superiors to know how I spent my time and how I was helping the organization.

When you do this, bosses will have a clear understanding of your contributions when raises or promotions come up. If your boss does not want to receive it on a regular basis, put these records in a folder so you can easily access them when requested.

Most people will not do this. You can be one who does.

# Adaptability

*A Word about Bosses*
There are all kinds of bosses. Figuring out how to meet or adapt to their expectations can be quite a challenge, particularly when you are a new employee.

It is a fact that every boss has his or her own standards. In case you want to examine relationships with bosses in detail, check out these books:

Ball, Michael. *@ the Entry Level: On Survival, Success, & Your Calling as a Young Professional.* Los Angeles: Pure Play Press, 2003.

D'Alessandro, David. *Career Warfare: 10 Rules for Building a Successful Personal Brand and Fighting to Keep It.* New York: McGraw-Hill, 2004.

Dobson, Michael, and Deborah Singer. *Managing Up: 59 Ways to Build a Career-Advancing Relationship with Your Boss.* New York: AMACOM, 2000.

O'Connell, Brian. *The Career Survival Guide.* New York: McGraw-Hill, 2003.

One thing that is consistent with employers is the desire to like and trust the people they hire. If employers have comparable candidates applying for the same position, what do you think is the deciding factor? It is often, "Do I like this person? Do the personal characteristics I see cause me to take a chance on him or her?"

Concentrate on those areas that let bosses know they can count on you —the **12 Simple Ways** described in this book.

*You Will Initially Fail More Than You Succeed, and That's Okay*
Employers like to see the willingness to try. They are not worried about failure. In fact, in the beginning, you will probably fail more than succeed. That's okay.

> I think that, while you are in school, you are encouraged to ask questions and use those around you to figure out the best course of action. People in the workplace are busy and do not have time to baby-sit a college graduate or even a new employee. I remember finally realizing that it was better to try on my own and fail a bunch of times before wasting someone's time for, what is to them, a very simple question.
>
> **Ross Geisel**

People who are too worried about failing may be too cautious. They do just what is required. But that is not a way to get noticed or be given more responsibility.

Manager Brickman Allen with Laureate Education said, "Think out of the box. Don't do it the same way every time. Bring new ideas, and try new ways. Find out if they work or not."

Chris Hall said that new employees sometimes think of their supervisors as the ones "who can fire them." But most bosses want their employees to be successful. "The company doesn't want you to fail," Chris said.

As Brickman Allen put it, "The company hired me. They know what I'm doing. This organization must have confidence in me."

*Training*
Students and new employees with whom I spoke were very concerned about whether training would be available to them.

Managers at Laureate said there may not be training, but, once you realize what is not there, it is up to you to ask for it.

## Summary of Workplace Realities

- You will only get a few weeks a year off.
- You may not get training.
- You may be asked to do things that are "not in your job description."
- You will be asked to interrupt what you are doing for a more "urgent" job.
- Your solutions and ideas will probably not be greeted with enthusiasm right away.
- Something that was done yesterday may be thrown out of the window today.

- Less than excellent work is never okay.
- You won't necessarily be told how you are doing.
- Employers want to know you can follow first.

Notes_____

_____

_____

_____

_____

_____

_____

_____

_____

_____

_____

_____

_____

_____

_____

_____

_____

_____

_____

_____

_____

_____

_____

_____

# 19

# All Done...
# Bye-bye

Now that you've been through *Jumpstart Your Job*, you can see that all of the **12 Simple Ways** are essential for your success. Done collectively, they will create a positive impression about you. Done consistently, they will count.

You can be still in school, searching for a job, be a new employee, or an experienced worker. The **12 Simple Ways** will always matter to current and future employers.

This book is not meant to be a guarantee that you will be promoted or given challenging assignments. But when you practice the **12 Simple Ways,** your chances of moving ahead are enhanced.

As you finish this book and hopefully have practiced the **12 Simple Ways,** take the self-assessment one more time.

## Self-Assessment

**On a scale of 0 to 5, with 5 being something you do all the time, rate yourself on the following actions:**

| | |
|---|---|
| Do you smile when you greet people? | 0 1 2 3 4 5 |
| Do you look people in the eye when speaking to them? | 0 1 2 3 4 5 |
| Do you consider what might be appropriate dress before you go out? | 0 1 2 3 4 5 |
| Do you get work or school assignments done on time? | 0 1 2 3 4 5 |
| Are you on time to your job, class, a study group, or club meeting? | 0 1 2 3 4 5 |
| Do you return non-sales phone calls and e-mails no more than 12 to 24 hours later? | 0 1 2 3 4 5 |
| Do you admit your mistakes? | 0 1 2 3 4 5 |
| Do you use proper grammar and avoid slang in a work or school setting? | 0 1 2 3 4 5 |
| Do you write thank-you notes? | 0 1 2 3 4 5 |
| Do you say thank you when someone does something for you? | 0 1 2 3 4 5 |
| Are you asked for your opinion? | 0 1 2 3 4 5 |
| Do you avoid complaining? | 0 1 2 3 4 5 |
| Do you avoid gossiping? | 0 1 2 3 4 5 |
| Do you help others, even when you would rather do something else? | 0 1 2 3 4 5 |
| Do your friends or coworkers ask you for help? | 0 1 2 3 4 5 |
| Do you stop yourself from interrupting other people while they are speaking? | 0 1 2 3 4 5 |
| Do you actually hear what other people say before you respond? | 0 1 2 3 4 5 |

| | |
|---|---|
| Do other people ask you to be their mentor? | 0 1 2 3 4 5 |
| If you do not know how to do something that would make life easier for you, do you make it a priority to learn the skill you need? | 0 1 2 3 4 5 |
| Do you keep your word when you make a promise to do something? | 0 1 2 3 4 5 |
| **TOTAL** | |

## Scoring the Assessment

80–100  Fabulous! Pass this book along to friends, or reread when you need a boost.

60–79  You are already headed in the right direction. Practice the **12 Simple Ways** for even more success.

40–59  You are in the middle of the pack, and there are lots of ways to move up if you will practice the **12 Simple Ways**.

20–39  Some red flags are being raised. Fortunately, to remedy this, go back over the **12 Simple Ways**.

0–19  Help is always available to you. In addition to practicing the **12 Simple Ways**, talk with a counselor or trusted friend for advice.

How did you do this time? If you still need to work on some of the **12 Simple Ways**, make a commitment!

At the end of the day, it is all about what people perceive about you. Do they say, "I can count on her" or "I can trust him"? Or is it, "I *wonder* if I can count on her or trust him"?

Reputation counts.

# Appendix

## Books

Baber, Anne, and Lynne Waymon. *Make Your Contacts Count.* New York: AMACOM, 2002.
•   One of the very best books there is about networking

Ball, Michael. *@ the Entry Level: On Survival, Success, & Your Calling as a Young Professional.* Los Angeles: Pure Play Press, 2003.
•   What you can expect
•   Dealing with bosses

Canfield, Jack, and Janet Switzer. *The Success Principles: How to Get from Where You Are to Where You Want to Be.* New York: Harper Collins, 2005.
•   Strategies to build your confidence
•   Tackling daily challenges

Carlson, Richard, PhD. *The Don't Sweat Guide for Graduates.* New York: Don't Sweat Press, 2002.
•   Transition from college to workplace
•   Professional/personal life balance

Coplin, Bill. *10 Things Employers Want You to Learn in College.* Berkeley, CA.: Ten Speed Press, 2003.
•   Skills you can develop

- Classes to take
- Resources
- Job interview tips

Corcodilos, Nick A. *Ask the Headhunter: Reinventing the Interview to Win the Job*. New York: Penguin Group, 1997.
- What employers want
- Job interview preparation

Covey, Stephen. *The 7 Habits of Highly Effective People*. New York: Free Press, 2004.
- Personal and professional effectiveness

D'Alessandro, David. Career *Warfare: 10 Rules for Building a Successful Personal Brand and Fighting to Keep It*. New York: McGraw-Hill, 2004.
- Building your reputation
- What bosses want

DePhillips, Susan. *Corporate Confidential: What It Really Takes to Get to the Top*. Avon, MA.: Platinum Press, 2005.
- What you need to do to get ahead on the job

Dimitrius, Jo-Ellan, and Mark Mazzarella. *Put Your Best Foot Forward: Make a Great Impression By Taking Control of How Others See You*. New York: Scribner, 2000.
- Qualities of a great impression
- Physical appearance and body language
- Communication skills

Dobson, Michael, and Deborah Singer. *Managing Up: 59 Ways to Build a Career-Advancing Relationship with Your Boss*. New York: AMACOM, 2000.
- Building a good relationship with your boss

Freedman, Elizabeth. *Work 101: Learning the Ropes of the Workplace without Hanging Yourself.* New York: Delta Trade Paperback, 2007.
- Business etiquette
- Effective communication tips

Green, Marianne Ehrlich. *Internship Success.* Chicago: VGM Career Horizons, 1997.
- Landing an internship and making the most of the experience

Gustafson, Kristen. *Graduate: Everything You Need to Succeed after College.* Herndon, VA: Capital Books, 2002.
- Written by a college graduate from 1998
- Transition from college to workplace

Hawk, Barbara Spencer. *What Employers Really Want: The Insider's Guide to Getting a Job.* Chicago: VGM Career Horizons, 1998.
- Job search
- Qualities employers want
- How to write résumés
- Job interview strategies

Healy, Kent, and Kyle Healy. *"Cool Stuff"* ™ *they should teach in school.* San Clemente, CA.: "Cool Stuff" Media, 2005.
- Real-world information for teens and young adults

Holton, Ed. *The Ultimate New Employee Survival Guide.* Princeton, NJ: Peterson's, 1998.
- Transition from college to work
- Challenges of first job
- Bosses
- Organizational cultures

Holton, Elwood F., and Sharon S Naquin. *How to Succeed in Your First Job: Tips for New College Graduates.* San Francisco: Berrett-Koehler Publishers, Inc. 2001.

- College experience versus workplace
- Moving beyond the newcomer status

Jedding, Kenneth. *Real Life Notes: Reflections and Strategies for Life after Graduation.* New York: Double Rose Books, 2002.
- Transition from college to workplace
- Career planning and decisions

Joyce, Amy. *I Went to College for This?* New York: McGraw Hill, 2003.
- Work realities
- What behaviors matter
- Advice from twenty-something career columnist from *The Washington Post*

Karsh, Brad. *Confessions of a Recruiting Director: A Top Recruiter Reveals Why He Said No to Thousands of Candidates—And How You Can Get the Yes.* New York: Prentice Hall Press, 2006.
- Tips to getting hired

Knight, Rebecca. *A Car, Some Cash and a Place to Crash: The Only Post-College Survival Guide You'll Ever Need.* United States: Rodale, 2003.
- Written by a college graduate from 1998
- Advice from young professionals

Kravetz, Stacy. *Welcome to the Real World: You've Got an Education, Now Get a Life.* New York: W. W. Norton & Company, Inc. 2004.
- Transition from college to workplace
- Job search

Levit, Alexandra. *They Don't Teach Corporate in College: A Twenty-Something's Guide to the Business World.* Franklin Lakes, NJ: Career Press, 2004.
- Written by a college graduate from 1998
- Advice for college seniors and recent college graduates about the corporate world

Liang, Jengyee. *Hello Real World! A Student's Approach to Great Internships, Co-ops and Entry Level Positions.* North Charleston, SC: BookSurge Publishing, 2006.
- Internship and job search advice from author's perspective

Malinchak, James. *From College to the Real World.* Montrose, CA: Positive Publishing, 1995.
- Internships
- Networking
- Creating résumés that are read
- Cover letters
- Interviewing tips

Masters, Andy. *Life after College: What to Expect and How to Succeed in Your Career.* Hawthorn Publishing, 2005.
- Career planning and decisions
- Relationships with boss
- Organizational skills

Maysonave, Sherry. *Casual Power: How to Power Up Your Nonverbal Communication and Dress Down for Success.* Austin: Bright Books, 1999.
- Illustrations of business casual attire for men and women

O'Connell, Brian. *The Career Survival Guide.* New York: McGraw-Hill, 2003.
- Office politics
- Recognizing company culture
- Bosses
- Mentors

Robbins, Alexandra, and Abby Wilner. *Quarterlife Crisis.* New York: Jeremy P. Tarcher/Putnam, 2001.
- Transition from college to workplace
- College experience versus real world
- Professional/personal life balance

Sanders, Tim. *The Likeability Factor: How to Boost Your L-Factor and Achieve Your Life's Dreams*. New York: Crown Publishers, 2005.
• Personality traits

Sindell, Milo, and Thuy Sindell. *Sink or Swim!: New Job. New Boss. 12 Weeks to Get It Right*. Avon, MA: Adams Media Corporation, 2006.
• Understanding the company culture
• Workplace priorities

Students Helping Students. *Have No Career Fear: A College Grad's Guide to Snagging Work, Blazing a Career Path, and Reaching Job Nirvana*. New York: Prentice Hall Press, 2005.
• Tips for getting jobs from students

Templar, Richard. *The Rules of Work*. Upper Saddle River, NJ: Prentice Hall, 2005.
• Important behaviors for the job

Trunk, Penelope. *Brazen Careerist: The New Rules for Success*. New York: Warner Business Books, 2007.
• Career advice and strategies for Generations X and Y
• Office politics
• Bosses

Useroff, Roz. *Customize Your Career: How to Develop a Winning Strategy to Move Up, Move Ahead, or Move On*. New York: McGraw-Hill, 2004.
• Tips for success on the job

Vogt, Peter. *Career Wisdom for College Students: Insights You Won't Get in Class, on the Internet or from Your Parents*. New York: Facts On File, 2007.
• Career advice
• Career decision-making tips

# Online Resources

People sometimes think they will be offered job interviews and jobs if they post their résumé online. This is not realistic. The following sites listed are some of the best, but do not guarantee you will find a job. Use all Internet sites with care.

AfterCollege (www.thejobresource.com)
- Internships and part-time and full-time jobs posted by state
- Career resources
- Ability to post résumé

Ask the Headhunter® (www.asktheheadhunter.com)
- Can post job search questions that are answered online

Career Builder.com (www.careerbuilder.com)
- Post résumés
- Job seeker advice and articles
- Notification of career fairs
- Job alerts via e-mail

Careers.org (www.careers.org)
- Job search
- Resource lists

CollegeGrad.com (www.collegegrad.com)
- Job search advice
- Career resources such as short-term medical insurance information
- Help with résumés/cover letters
- Employer research
- Job postings

CollegeRecruiter.com (www.collegerecruiter.com)
- Site for college students and recent graduates
- Ask the experts
- Thoughts from recent graduates
- Job search

HotJobs (www.hotjobs.com)
- Job search by industry and state
- Résumé posting
- Calculate salaries

JobHuntersBible.com (www.jobhuntersbible.com)
- Recommends best sites for job openings, where to post résumés, get salary information, and research companies
- Site supplements *What Color Is Your Parachute* by Dick Bolles

Job Search News.com (www.jobsearchnews.com)
- Job search newsletters and career columnists appearing in magazines and newspapers
- Can ask questions
- Current job search trends and career advice

JobWeb (www.jobweb.com)
- For college students and new college graduates
- Job search advice
- Employer search
- Salary information
- Owned and sponsored by the National Association of Colleges and Employers

Monster.com (www.monster.com)
- Career advice and assistance, including virtual interviews, job profiles, salary negotiation tips, and résumés/cover letters
- Can post résumé
- For internship information, go to www.monstertrak.monster.com

Quintessential Careers (www.quintcareers.com)
- Includes a link to www.mycareerblast.com, a comprehensive site for college students
- Job search articles

- Career-related advice
- Résumés
- Cover sheets
- Job board

The Riley Guide (www.rileyguide.com)
- Lists many job search sites and services

Vault (www.vault.com)
- Graduate school information
- Job search
- Surveys
- Job advice
- Links to Vault Europe and Vault Asia

# About the Author

Marcia Hall, founder of Reputation COUNTS, has more than 25 years of experience working with the business community, particularly in her role as executive director of a leading chamber of commerce in Maryland. She is the award-winning author of *Navigating Newbie-ism: 12 Simple Ways to Thrive in Your First Job and Career, The College Student's Guide.*

Marcia presents workshops about building your reputation and effective networking. She can be reached at www.reputationcounts.com.

*If you would like to:*

- Sign up for free workplace tips

- Hear interviews from employers who tell you what behaviors are most important to demonstrate

- Take the Self Assessment Quiz, "Do you have the necessary personal attributes to succeed on the job?"

*Go to:*
## www.reputationcounts.com

For additional copies of *Jumpstart Your Job*,
order online at www.reputationcounts.com

9 780978 806644